IMAGES
of England

ISLEWORTH:
THE SECOND SELECTION

Mr John Lee (1866-1927). Well known as a greengrocer of No. 3 Upper Square (see page 32), Mr Lee is shown here in his uniform as a member of the Isleworth Volunteer Fire Brigade. He was the driver of the engine and it was said that 'although not a giant in stature, few men could "handle the ribbons" or control horses like Mr Lee.'

IMAGES
of England

ISLEWORTH:
THE SECOND SELECTION

Compiled by
Mary and Kevin Brown

TEMPUS

First published 1998
Copyright © Mary and Kevin Brown, 1998

Tempus Publishing Limited
The Mill, Brimscombe Port,
Stroud, Gloucestershire, GL5 2QG

ISBN 0 7524 1501 8

Typesetting and origination by
Tempus Publishing Limited
Printed in Great Britain by
Midway Clark Printing, Wiltshire

This book is dedicated to those who have previously recorded life in Isleworth, in writing or illustration, and to those who have shared their memories with us.

'Coon Concert Party' and 'Tennessee Girls', 1920s. Before the growth of television and radio, most entertainment was locally organized. Concerts, dances, whist drives and amateur theatricals all abounded. Here, two local groups have combined to give a concert to raise money for charity. The 'Tennessee Dancing Girls' were organized by Miss Joyce Robinson, third from left on the back row, and the 'Coon Concert Party' was organized by local policeman Mr Bill Barber, fourth from left on the back row. They were accompanied by Mr Harry Goddard, at the extreme right.

Contents

Church Ferry, *c.* 1910. Dating from the reign of Henry VIII, this pedestrian ferry provided an important service giving access between the Middlesex and Surrey banks of the Thames. Even in the eighteenth century the nearest bridges (Kew, opened in 1759, and Richmond, opened in 1777, both originally toll bridges) were a good distance away.

Acknowledgements

The majority of the illustrations used in this book are taken from the authors' collection, and we would like to thank all those who, over the years, have allowed us to borrow photographs to copy or who have shared their memories of Isleworth with us. In particular we would like to thank the following people who have provided illustrations or information used in this book: Miss Doreen Ayres, Mrs Gilda Bagnall, Mrs Olive Beech, Mrs N. Betts, Miss M. Black, Mrs S. Branson, Mrs O. Breden, Mrs B. Bryan, Miss P. Burch, the late Lily Carter, Mrs T. Claudell, Mrs L. Chivers, Mrs L. Cleveland, Mr J. Cooper, the late Mr Ken Cooper, Mr Doug Cotterell, Mr G. Cox, Miss Doreen Dawson, Miss Marion Easton, Mrs B. Evans, Miss Jennifer Evans, the late Mr Jim Felton, the late Mr Alan Field, Mrs B. Field, the late Mrs Ena Field, Mrs Margaret Field and family, Mr P. Ford, Mr and Mrs H. Goddard, the late Miss D. Francis, Mrs M. Harnet, Miss I. Hawkins, 'Helsdons', Mrs A. Holt, Mrs D. Jackson, Mrs Ethel Jones, Mrs Joyce Lane, Mrs M. Lang, the late Mrs W. Maidment, the late Mr Ernie Manning, Miss E. Mayger, Mr and Mrs Middleditch and Mr C. Middleditch, Mr J. Middleton, Mr Midgley, Mrs I. Morris, Mrs G. Mulford, Mr and Mrs V. Murphy, Mrs Y. Oakes, Mrs J. Oates, Miss Joan Over, Mrs D. Pearce, Mrs S. Rahman, Mrs E. Reynolds, Mr 'Curly' Richardson, the landlord of the Royal Oak public house, the late Mr Geoffrey Sadler, St Mary's church Bridge Road, St Mary's church Osterley, Miss E. Taylor, Miss J. Temple, Mrs Theresa Turner, the late Mr F. Vicary, the late Mr P. Voller, Miss Gwen Weston, Mr Thomas White, Mr L. Wiles and the late Mr John Young. We should also like to thank the staff of the local studies department in Hounslow Library for their assistance while we were researching this book.

Introduction

There has probably been a settlement on the banks of the Thames at Isleworth for some 4,000 years, although the earliest surviving written record dates from 695 AD. The Domesday Book records the Manor of Isleworth, and mentions the presence of a priest, indicating that there was already a church in Isleworth or perhaps a chapel attached to the manor house. In 1415 the manor formed part of Henry V's endowment of the new Syon Monastery.

Isleworth's proximity to London and the royal palaces at Richmond and Hampton Court, together with the comparative ease of transport along the River Thames and the coaching road which followed the old Roman road to the West Country, led to the erection of a number of large houses for the nobility. Following the Dissolution of the Monasteries, Syon became Syon House, seat of the Duke of Northumberland, while other houses included Osterley House, Wyke House, Gumley House, Spring Grove House, Gordon House, St Margaret's House, Isleworth House, Worton Hall and Worton Manor.

The village itself, however, changed slowly. Most local employment was in agriculture, Isleworth being perfectly situated with good transport connections to supply market garden produce to the burgeoning population of London. In 1839 there were some thirty-two separate market gardens in Isleworth. Other employment centred on the River Thames – fishermen, lightermen, ferrymen, dock workers etc. – and in the mills producing flour, again for the London market.

The picture of a rural village, centred around the ancient parish church dedicated to All Saints and set in the midst of agricultural land, changed greatly in the late nineteenth and early twentieth centuries. As elsewhere around London the population increase has been enormous, housing has covered the agricultural land relentlessly with waves of building following the arrival of the railways and the opening of the Great West Road. Today Isleworth is part of one conurbation while the tiny hamlets which surrounded the old village are but place names on the map. The village continues to alter at a seemingly ever faster rate as development gives way to redevelopment. Change is continual and inevitable and as we record some of Isleworth's recent past we remember that today is tomorrow's history.

It was with some trepidation that we wrote our first book on Isleworth in the Archive Photographs Series, in 1995. How, we wondered, would the book be received? The response to that book was overwhelming from all generations; older residents recalled happy memories of times past, while younger readers were able to glimpse a vanished way of life. As a result of much prompting and encouragement we have again 'taken the plunge' and hope you like this book as much as the first. Although the two books are independent, this work is intended to complement the first, and the opportunity has been taken to expand the coverage by including many subjects which, for want of space or suitable illustration, we were unable to include in the earlier work. There is some unavoidable overlap, for it would be impossible to produce a book of this nature without including some of the 'landmark' buildings of Isleworth – the Old Blue School, All Saints' church and the London Apprentice for example. While we have tried to be as comprehensive as possible, there are still some elusive buildings for which we have no suitable pictures – Heddon House, Mandeville House, and the old Royal Standard public house come to mind.

Once again we should like to thank all those who have so generously shared their memories of Isleworth with us, or who have lent us photographs to copy. We would be glad to receive further information about any of the illustrations reproduced here and hope that there will be something in this book to interest everyone.

All Saints' Missionary Play, 1928. Members of All Saints' Sunday school and choir wore national costumes from around the world to perform a missionary play in the old church hall behind South Street. The play toured local churches, organized by the curate, Revd Merryfield, standing on the right at the back, and the organist, Miss Tester, seated extreme right. Among those shown are: Winnie Hill – Burmese girl; Olive Hill – Indian girl; Kathie Brooks – Indian girl; Ethel Middleton – peasant girl; Vera Hills – shepherd; Doris Argent – Chinese girl; and Maggie Merry – Chinese girl. Also in the picture are Mari Butt, Rosa Robeson, Jack Stevens, Eileen King, Mrs Woolford and Freda Woolford. One participant still recalls the event, even to the hymns sung: *Abide with me* and *God is working his purpose out*. All Saints' parish hall was erected on the ground between the mission church (see page 37) and the South Street shops. The foundation stone was laid by the Duke of Northumberland on 25 November 1922 and the dedication of the completed hall by the Bishop of Kensington took place on 23 June 1923. Access to the hall was through an alley between the South Street shops, and a wide passage through the hall gave access to the mission church. During the war the parish hall was requisitioned by military authorities, but it was mainly used for parish events and church organizations. The mission church was demolished in the 1960s and the parish hall in the 1980s. The Blue School's new hall, opened in 1986, now occupies the site of both buildings.

One

Isleworth:
The Old Village

Situated on the banks of the Thames, the village of Isleworth grew around the parish church of All Saints and the manor house. In 1415 the manor formed part of Henry V's endowment of Syon Monastery. After the Dissolution, the monastery site was developed as Syon House, becoming the seat of the Dukes of Northumberland, and the village gradually changed as the old manorial ties lessened, and new employment opportunities arose.

Syon House, 1903. Built in around 1550 on the site of the former Syon Monastery, the house is now the seat of the Duke of Northumberland. Much of the interior was re-designed by Robert Adam in the 1760s. The lion, badge of the Percy family, surmounting the building was brought to Syon from Northumberland House on the Strand when that building was demolished in 1874. Set in magnificent parkland overlooking the Thames, the house is now open to the public.

Syon Park, *c.* 1910. Children from a local Sunday school are gathered for their annual outing. Such events included races and games with prizes for all, a picnic tea and probably a bun or orange to take home. They were simple pleasures, but more meaningful when people had less material wealth.

The Great Conservatory, Syon Park, *c.* 1917. It was designed by Charles Fowler and built between 1820 and 1827. The gardens of Syon have been a notable feature of the estate since the 1540s when Dr W. Turner, the 'father of English botany', laid out a botanic garden. Notable gardeners later employed here include T. Hoy and W. Forsythe – the plants hoya and forsythia are named after them. Between 1750 and 1770 Capability Brown laid out a large area of the grounds which are today open to the public.

Syon House, seen across the river from the towpath on the Surrey bank, *c.* 1905. The smartly dressed couple are strolling towards Richmond and have nearly reached the steps opposite All Saints' church where they could hail the ferryman to cross the river. Given the muddy towpath one wonders how practical the long dress was – but perhaps she did not have to do her own laundry!

Church Ferry, *c.* 1900. Mr Charlie Simmons, ferryman at Isleworth for over forty years, stands in the ferry boat by the church steps awaiting passengers.

The river front in 1905. In the centre is the London Apprentice, first recorded as a public house in 1731. Note the floating boathouse operated by E. Finn, 'boat builder, boats to let', and the wide slipway allowing horse drawn carts easy access to the foreshore to unload cargo from barges.

The wedding of Thomas White and Violet Gosling at All Saints' church, 2 October 1929. 'Tom' White, like his father, was a watchmaker, and the family business was based at 41 South Street from 1902 to 1967. Tom White became a prominent member of his profession and he certified watches for government, police and sports organizations. In his spare time he was involved in the popular sport of bicycle racing, both as participant and time-keeper, and friends from the Ross Wheelers Cycle Club have formed a guard of honour holding bicycle wheels aloft. The wedding was held on a Wednesday, then half-day closing in Isleworth. Few people could get time off work to marry and registers show weddings taking place at holiday times – even Christmas Day – or on half-day closing as the newly weds were expected back at work the following day.

Isleworth Rowing Club, 1930. The River Thames has played a large part in Isleworth's history, providing a highway for communication and much employment in the various wharves, docks etc. The river has also long been used for leisure purposes. In 1924 Isleworth Rowing Club was formed, with a nucleus of eight men. The club headquarters was a floating boathouse moored by the London Apprentice. Members competed against rival clubs along the Thames, participated in the annual Isleworth Regatta, and the club produced a number of international rowers. Sadly the club ceased to exist in the early 1940s, and later attempts to revive the regatta did not prove to be viable. Those pictured are, left to right, back row: Messrs A. Pishorn, G. Carr, S. McCarthy, J. Brown, D. Scrivener, H. Lock, C. Richmond, A. Brown, F. Worsley, L. Gerrard, W. Shiers, G. Nutley, L. Ryder, J. Bolton. Third row: F. McCarthy, A. Leader, F. Lawrence, G. Henderson, C. Morey, A. Bond, C. McCarthy (vice-captain), V. Griffiths, C. Arnold, A. Phipps, A. Turner, L. Dunham, G. Hill, H. Phipps, R. McCarthy, J. Pearce. Second row: Misses E. Wareham, M. Cöver, L. Harris, D. Ward, D. Cooper, K. Ward, G. Smith, A. Tompkins, E. Young, P. Blight, K. Davis (vice-captain), J. Chapman (financial secretary), M. Blight (secretary), D. Lambard, M. Major, L. Burman, P. Taylor, N. Chandler. Front row: Messrs S.T. Allen (treasurer), A.T. Green (VP), M.A. Thurlow (coach), H. Webster (VP), A.T. Hare (VP), P.W. Bumstead (vice-chairman), E.C. Young (captain), Prier Wotton (president), Miss G. Chapman (captain), F.G. Pearson (chairman), W.J. Tucker (VP), Cllr A. Dennis (VP), S. Coates (VP), T. Griffith (VP), J.C. Young (honorary secretary).

Church Street, c. 1880. On the right is All Saints' parish church, formerly a medieval stone building matching the surviving tower. This was rebuilt in brick in 1705-6 using a modified Wren design. In 1866-67 a chancel was added, the portion not ivy-clad in this picture. To the left of the church is Porch House, sometimes called Stone House. This was built around 1706 using stone salvaged when the church was rebuilt. Porch House extended right across Church Street pavement, with access to the church and churchyard through an arched passageway, the top of which can be seen in the picture. Porch House was let and the income used for charitable purposes. Among the tenants was a Mrs Fowler who paid £10 for a year's rent in 1743. She so liked the spot that her tomb was erected below her dressing room window against the churchyard boundary wall. Other notable residents have included Revd Dacre Craven, William Ivory and Count Jarsheing, envoy from the king of Denmark. On several occasions Porch House was used as a private school and in 1808 the Beadle was sent to complain to Mr Lockwood that his scholars were continually breaking the windows in the vestry room. To the left of Porch House are the buildings in Church Street with the London Apprentice on the extreme left. Outside the London Apprentice stands a white hooded wagon used to bring gunpowder to Curtis & Harvey's gunpowder wharf in Church Street – the horses were shod in copper to avoid sparks. Also note the floating boathouse and the ferryman in mid-stream.

Porch House, Church Street, c. 1880. An enlargement from the picture opposite. Built around 1706, by the late nineteenth century the building had deteriorated to such an extent that the local authority condemned it as being unsound and dangerous. Consequently the building was partially demolished in 1892, and a flight of steps constructed to give access to the churchyard and church from Church Street roadway. The site remained empty until 1903 when it was sold by order of the trustees of the Isleworth Parochial Charities. Two cottages were then erected on the site (see picture below). In 1969 these were converted into one residence with a mock gothic façade, called Butter Field House.

The river front, 1913. To the left of All Saints' church stand the two cottages erected on the site of the Porch House. In front of the cottages can be seen the end of Isleworth Ait, then used to grow osiers for basket making. The ait is now a nature reserve and covered with more mature trees. Note the barges on the foreshore and the cart unloading timber. The white section on the two mooring posts show the high tide water line.

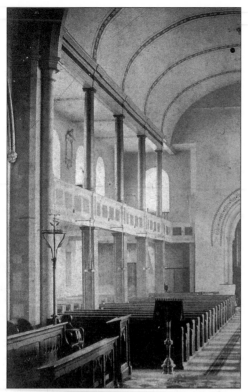

All Saints' church seen from the chancel arch looking towards the west door, c. 1875. The nave and galleries dated from the 1706 rebuilding, but the pews were altered in 1866-67 when the chancel was also added. Previously the seating had been box pews but the changes allowed some 270 extra seats to be added so that the church could 'now contain about 1,000 persons comfortably'. The original 1706 barrel roofing was quite simply decorated as seen here, but in 1888 a subscription was raised locally to decorate the ceiling and walls. Sadly the church was destroyed by arson in 1943.

Isleworth church Sunday school pupils and helpers are gathered for their 'Annual Treat', 29 June 1888. This was held in the grounds of Isleworth House, now part of the Nazareth House complex but then the residence of Mrs McAndrew. Tea was provided in the Public Hall owing to inclement weather. Note the separate banners for the Brentford End Sunday school and Green School.

All Saints' parish workers in June 1888, seen in the grounds of 41 Church Street, then the vicarage and now a council hostel. The picture was taken for the Revd H.W.P. Richards who retired in August 1888 having been vicar of Isleworth for thirty-three years. During his incumbency the church chancel had been added and the 'iron' church, later to become All Souls', had been established at St Margaret's. Among those in the picture are members of All Saints' and the 'iron' church choirs, district visitors, staff of the Green School, Blue School, North Street National School (the girls' department of the Blue School), Sunday school teachers, committee members of the Church of England Temperance Society and Band of Hope, sidesmen, churchwardens and the two curates, G.T. Andrews and Francis Gurdon. The Revd Richards is seated twelfth from the left, also seated are Miss C. Ashton (headmistress of the Green School, sixth from left), Miss Sarah Davies (National School infants' mistress, seventh from left) and her sister Miss Emily Davies (headmistress of the National School, ninth from left). Alfred Prior, headmaster of the Blue School, is standing in the back row, two to the right of the top-hatted gentlemen.

Jacob Crawther (1783-1863) was for many years associated with All Saints' Parish church. In 1828 he was appointed to the post of Beadle, becoming parish clerk in 1844, a post he held until his death in 1863 at which time he was receiving the salary of £16 per year. This was an important post at a time when many areas of local government, from education to drainage and highway maintenance, were the responsibilities of the local parish. In addition to his parish duties he was 'a prominent official at church services and occupied a pulpit position, making and leading responses and all terminating "Amens" in a loud voice'. He is buried in All Saints' churchyard.

The river front, 1909. The Thames has played an important part in Isleworth's history, both as a means of transport and source of employment. Here we see some of the many sailing barges which constantly visited Isleworth which was then regarded as a port in its own right, complete with a customs officer. The boy on the extreme left is said to be 'Con' Dargon, who later became a ferryman at Isleworth.

James Love (1788-1862) was appointed Parish Beadle in 1844 as successor to Jacob Crawther (see opposite). At that date his duties were described as 'to assist to open the pew doors, to prevent irregularities in the churchyard, to give notice to the coroner in cases of sudden death, to attend all parochial meetings, to execute the orders of the churchwardens and overseers, to serve precepts from the High Constable and to act as public crier'; for these duties he received £15 per year, with a suit of clothes every two years. This consisted of 'a blue coat with gold edging around the collar, a black waistcoat and velveteen breeches and a hat with gold lace band', and in addition he carried a staff of office. He is seen here out of uniform, but must have been an imposing figure as he strode around Isleworth collecting the parish and poor rates and enforcing the churchwardens' orders. He lived in Phoenix Row where, in addition to his official duties, he was also a greengrocer.

The river front in the late 1950s. The cranes and barges show this still to be a busy commercial port. Note the first floor bay window added to the London Apprentice in 1906.

Bridge Wharf, *c.* 1950. Founded in 1903, H. Taylor & Son became one of Isleworth's most prominent companies, operating as wharfingers, warehousemen and haulage contractors, transporting building supplies, animal feed, coal, carbon black, rubber and general merchandise. Six ships operated cross-channel trade and the company had over a million cubic feet of warehouse space in Isleworth, some of it heated to soften rubber before being transferred to factories. Here a warehouse and part of the company's fleet of lorries can be seen.

Mill Bridge, Church Street, 1907. The tall building on the left is Kidd's Mill, with the railings around the Mill Basin. Right of the picture is the Orange Tree public house, which dated from the early eighteenth century and had a notable panelled upper room. The pub closed early this century and was subsequently used as offices for Kidd's Mill and then Taylor's Wharf before becoming a private residence. It has since been demolished.

Kidd's Flour Mill, *c*. 1920, with part of the fleet of steam lorries operated by the mill. Kidd's Mill was the last in a succession of mills to occupy this site from Tudor times. Mills were erected here in 1543, rebuilt in 1669, burnt down in 1795 and repaired in 1804. Shortly afterwards the lease passed to Richard and Benjamin Kidd and then to their brother Samuel. Under Samuel Kidd and his successors the mill expanded greatly, becoming one of the largest and most modern in the London area. In 1846 two steam engines were added to supplement the water power. By 1887, twenty-nine pairs of millstones and eleven sets of rollers were producing some 3,000 sacks of flour every week and Kidd's Mill was a major local employer. Local residents still recall, as children, collecting 'test bake' loaves from the Mill or carrying home bags of flour in their dolls' prams. Samuel Kidd was a Quaker and supported many local charities. He is also known to have supplied flour to the poor of Isleworth during the period of the potato famine in the 1840s and the economic depression of the 1850s. He was also active in the London Master Bakers' Pensions and Almshouse Society. Although he retired in 1863 the company continued to be known as Samuel Kidd & Co. until it closed in 1934. The buildings were demolished in 1941, thought the Mill Basin and mill race can still be seen.

Alterations being made to Mill House, July 1869. First recorded in 1818, Mill House stood off Mill Plat, between Warkworth House and Church Street. For many years it provided offices for the mill, as well as accommodation for the mill manager. One manager was Patrick Murphy, who lived there for fifty years. The house was demolished in 1909 and today part of Millside Place is on the site.

Dundee House, a Georgian building which stood in Mill Plat, late 1960s. The name may derive from Captain Dundee who lived there in the 1850s, although little is known of him. A succession of residents followed until 1906 when the house was purchased to house young children from Percy House School. Dundee House later became a hostel for the homeless under Hounslow Council. This closed in the late 1960s and the building, having become 'squalid and semi-derelict' was demolished soon afterwards. The site is now part of West Middlesex Hospital grounds.

Elizabeth Cottage, Mill Plat, late 1960s. Built in the early nineteenth century, Elizabeth Cottage stood opposite the alley leading to North Street. Another alley formerly ran by the side of Elizabeth Cottage behind the hospital through to Park Road. Officially known as Union Lane, this was locally called Cut Throat Alley, as it had an unsavoury reputation! Elizabeth Cottage has been demolished and the site is now part of the hospital grounds.

Mrs Blanche Pike sitting by a newly erected Anderson shelter in the garden of 23 Silverhall Street, 1940. Named after Sir John Anderson (Home Secretary in 1939-40), Anderson shelters were small, prefabricated air-raid shelters partly buried in people's gardens and covered with earth. Many people slept in these shelters nightly during the Blitz, while others only took shelter during air raids.

Mrs Mary E. Curtis in the late 1940s. Mary was a well known character remembered for having odd-coloured eyes, who for many years ran the general stores at No. 19 North Street, at the corner of Percy Gardens. Opening hours were long: 8 a.m. to 8 p.m. Monday to Saturday and 8 a.m. to 1 p.m. on Sunday. Most business was by credit, each customer having a book where purchases were entered, and payment was made on a Saturday, the usual pay day. Mrs Curtis was popular with all the local people who clubbed together to present her with a house-coat and slippers when she retired, hence the photograph.

North Street, *c.* 1960. On the right is the entrance to Percy Gardens, showing the corner shop run for many years by Mrs M. Curtis. Though listed as part of North Street, this short terrace was originally built and numbered as Nos 1-5 Percy Gardens.

The Duke's River behind 18 Percy Gardens, *c.* 1930. Percy Gardens residents were responsible for maintaining and shoring up the banks of the Duke of Northumberland's River where it bordered Percy Gardens. There was no National Rivers Authority or Environment Agency then! Pausing for the photographer are Mr G. Manning, Mr A. Baily and Mr B. Williams. Beyond the river is part of the rear of Ingrams Almshouses in Mill Plat.

Percy Gardens, *c.* 1960. This mid nineteenth-century terrace off North Street was compulsorily purchased in 1961 and demolished. Now flats also called Percy Gardens occupy the site. At the end of the terrace, beyond the Duke's River can be seen part of West Middlesex Hospital. The low front garden walls were originally topped with ornamental railings which were removed for wartime recycling.

Blue School, North Street, *c.* 1950, built in 1879 to house the school's girls' department. In 1939 the boys also moved here from the old school building in Lower Square. The building remained in use until the present building, also in North Street, opened in July 1960.

Blue School, North Street, *c.* 1920. Flag-waving pupils celebrate Empire Day outside the entrance to the infants' department. The school's infants' department was founded in North Street in 1829 by Mrs Kidd of the Isleworth Flour Mills. In the background are houses in Percy Gardens.

Blue School pupils dressed to represent nursery rhyme characters for classroom entertainment, *c.* 1916. This photograph was taken by Stanley Nixon, the South Street photographer.

Blue School infants, c. 1916. Posing for the photographer are, left, to right back row: Rosa Ingram, ? Butt, Tommy Griffin, Elsie Mayger, Rosa Pusey, ? Butt, ? Ingram, ? Prichard, Roy Bishop, Iris French and Lavinia Chittingdon. Front row: ? Flood, ? Prescott, ? Prescott, ? Manning, ? Vigor.

Lower Square, 1903. To the right is the old Blue School, built in 1841 and in use as a school until 1939. On the left is the Northumberland Arms, built in 1834. Below the Street lamp the sign advertises 'Wm. Lee, Son & Co. Limited, Lime Burners and Cement Manufacturers'; Eastwood later occupied this site. As ever, the photographer has attracted a group of interested onlookers.

Blue School pupils visiting the Festival Hall, 1957. Left to right, standing: Barry Butler, Peter Felton, Christine Brenchley, Brian Cole, Richard Goodhew, Gail Hay, Mrs Baker, Margaret Hancock, Michael Owen, Diana Buckingham, Hew Edwards, Elaine Marshall (?), Janet Hadley, Ian Maclean, Miss Savage, Ian Major. Kneeling: Pat Jones, Wendy Jenrick, Jane Call, Jeannette Felton, Jill Miller, Felicity May, Barry Wooler (?), Barry Morgan, Laurie Way and Clive Sheridan.

Lower Square, late 1950s. Houses between North Street and Lower Square have been demolished, leaving the Northumberland Arms, built in 1834, standing in isolation. Props support the eighteenth-century John Day House and the area has a general air of neglect as it awaits the redevelopment of the 1980s.

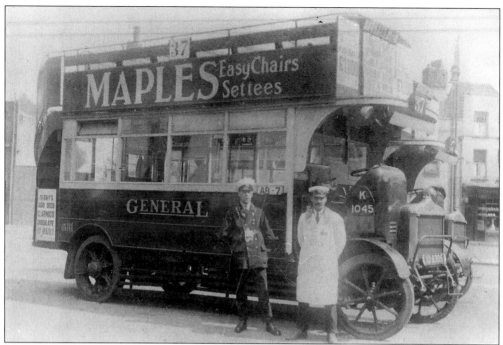

Lower Square in 1926, with an open-topped No. 37 bus with conductor and driver Mr J. Ward (in the white coat). From 1912 to 1920 the route ran between Peckham and Isleworth, terminating in Lower Square outside the Northumberland Arms. From 1920 the route extended to Hounslow on some services. Note the solid tyres and starting handle.

A side show at Isleworth Fair, c. 1935. Until the 1940s Isleworth held an annual fair on the first Monday in July. Lower Square and the Phoenix Yard were filled with roundabouts, swings, boxing booths, hoopla, Punch and Judy, fortune tellers etc. Stalls sold humbugs and candy-floss, hot potatoes and chestnuts, with 'all the fun of the fair'. Seen here is Mrs Evans with her daughters, Milly and Tilly, and their skittles stall.

Lower Square, said to be during Isleworth peace celebrations, 1919. Interested onlookers gather round a Scout band and revellers in fancy dress. At the top right is part of the old Blue School with a horse-drawn dray heavily laden with schoolchildren in front. At top left, open-topped No. 37 buses stand outside the Northumberland Arms. Buses turned here before going back to Putney.

Lynton Place, Nos 6, 8 and 10 North Street, c. 1960. Many houses from the last century were given names such as Lynton Place, Glenthorn Villas, Bounty Cottages etc., the result of piecemeal building as land became available or as developers' funds permitted. Regular street numbering was a later addition. Lynton Place was demolished shortly after this photograph was taken and the site became a car park. Subsequently the new British Legion was erected at the back of this site.

Nos 2 and 3 Upper Square, c. 1910. No. 2, with the shutters down, was William Hillier's fishmonger's and No. 3 John Lee's greengrocer's. In addition to selling fruit, vegetables, and flowers John Lee advertised a 'waggonette to let for private parties', 'coals and coke carted at lowest wharf prices' and 'covered vans for the removal of furniture and luggage'. He also sold coal in 14lb bags as many people could not afford to buy larger quantities.

Isleworth Cycle Stores, run by Mr William Hills, at 5 Upper Square, 1923. As well as selling bicycles and accessories, Mr Hill hired cycles out. He also repaired shoes, hence the nugget polish advertisement. In the doorway from left to right are Lizzie Rokins, Winnie Hill and Olive Hill. Mrs Rokins made toffee apples, selling them from her back door in Swan Street; if the apples were small two or three would go on a single stick.

Members of Isleworth fire brigade on their horse-drawn engine in Upper Square, c. 1914. The tallest building behind is the Castle public house with Thomas Peters' confectionery shop to the left and Alfred Haley, wardrobe dealer, to the right. The many-paned window marks Charles Blackaby, boot maker: 'All kinds of repairs executed.'

Demolition of Nos 15, 16 and 17 Upper Square in the 1950s, prior to 'straightening' the Richmond Road junction. In the centre, boarded up, is No. 17, T.H. Pratt's tobacconist shop, with the Castle public house on the right. On the extreme left stands Barclays Bank, closed in 1993 and now a travel agent's, while in the background stands Nazareth House convent and children's home, now an old people's home.

Demolition of Nos 15 to 17 Upper Square, 1950s. After the road junction was straightened, this site became a car park for the Castle and more recently an extension to the pub. On the extreme right are the offices of Lion Wharf and in the centre is Barclays Bank. Between these the doorway gave access to Shrewsbury Place where the old Roman Catholic chapel stood before St Bridget's church opened.

Edward Beck (1833-1913), a prominent member of the family which for many years owned Beck's Wharf, which later became Lion Wharf. They ran a fleet of sailing boats named for different virtues – *Faith, Hope, Charity, Concord, Felicity* etc. – which were used to bring building supplies of timber, lime, slate, cement and stone and also coal to the wharf at Isleworth. They also employed lath renderers and pit sawyers to convert the raw materials into the finished product for sale to local builders. Edward Beck lived at Heddon House on the Twickenham Road. He was a notable Quaker and is buried in the Quaker burial ground near Busch Corner.

Mr William Tucker with his daughter, Lucy, behind the counter of his pawnbroker's shop at 5-7 South Street, 1923. He also bought and sold second-hand goods and any unredeemed pledges would be sold from the shop. Lucy Tucker later ran 'Lucille's', the drapers on the Twickenham Road.

The Duke of Northumberland laying the foundation stone of All Saints' parish hall, 25 November 1922. The Duchess had been due to perform the ceremony but was prevented by illness, and so the Duke acted in her place. The stone, however, being carved in advance, erroneously recorded that the Duchess performed the ceremony.

A performance of *Cinderella* in All Saints' parish hall, *c.* 1950. Among the cast at this amateur theatrical are, left to right, far back: Eric Creighton, Brian Menzies. Standing: Ken Richards, -?-, Doug Holloway, Doreen Winterborne, Betty Winterborne, Joan Prince, Ron Brooks, Muriel Goode, Brian Gooding. Kneeling: Jackie Simpson, Margaret Gray, Margaret Kerr, -?-, Rita Atkins, Joyce Willis, and Janice Simpson. The wigs were unofficially 'borrowed' from the Law Courts.

First Isleworth Brownies on pack holiday in the late 1950s. Left to right, back row: -?-, Adrienne Beech, -?-, Sylvia Buffham (Brown Owl), -?-, -?-. Middle row: Margaret Allard, Sonia Kemp, Elizabeth Allard, Jacqueline Wortley, Jacqueline Collier, Lyn Tyrrell. Front Row: Sharon Tyrrell, Yverne Jones, Carol Webber, -?-, Elaine Webber, Margaret Ion. The pack is attached to All Saints' church.

Isleworth mission church, *c*. 1915. The Isleworth Mission was founded in 1910 by the Revd W.M. Rapson, a former Methodist minister. In 1913 the mission church was built by private subscription on land behind South Street where Stafford Place, a notorious slum, formerly stood. In 1915 the mission church was attached to All Saints' although the Revd Rapson continued as missioner, being ordained into the Church of England in 1916.

The Revd William Marsh Rapson together with helpers and thirty-one children of 'The Cradle Roll' outside the mission church in South Street, *c*. 1920. Wearing their Sunday best and with hands carefully folded they look a picture of innocence. The mission church was demolished in the 1960s and the adjoining Parish Hall in the 1980s. Today the Blue School New Hall occupies the site.

Upper Square, 3 October 1932. King's Watermen escort a Rolls-Royce conveying his Royal Highness the Duke of Gloucester and Charter Mayor, Councillor H.J. Nias, who toured the district following the presentation of the Charter of Incorporation for the newly formed Borough of Heston and Isleworth. The ceremonial presentation took place on the Great West Road outside Firestone's factory where a plaque in the pavement still marks the spot.

Upper Square, 3 October 1932. Members of the Legion of Frontiersmen form part of the charter procession. The buildings decorated with flags and bunting are the Rose Tea Room and J. Lee's greengrocery. At centre right can be seen the Swan public house.

No. 32 South Street, *c.* 1914. John Cox stands in the doorway of his pork and general butcher's shop. Note the iron framework for hanging meat and the gas lamp. Before the advent of refrigeration meat was prepared for immediate use, and late in the day on Saturday reduced in price to clear. Specialities included faggots, pease pudding, black pudding and saveloys. The poster to the left advertises a whist drive and dance.

4 The Pavement, South Street, 1922. Mr and Mrs John Cox stand in the doorway of their butcher's shop with, left to right: 'Robin', Charlie Williams, George Cox – who followed his father into the business and retired around 1987 – and Henry Cox. Note the sawdust on the ground. The impressive display was probably for the Christmas market.

South Street, *c.* 1920. A brass band leads flag-waving schoolchildren towards the Twickenham Road in what is said to be a Remembrance Day parade. On the extreme left No. 60 was then a confectionery shop. The tall building was No. 54, for many years the surgery of Drs Scott and Cassels-Smith who practised here. Beyond, four cottages lay back from the road. In the farthest of these, No. 46, lived Alfred Rowles, the chimney sweep. He kept a slate by the garden gate for people to request visits – there was no answer phone then! The flag pole, extreme right, stood in front of the Kings Arms public house (off the picture), which was rebuilt in 1898, and often called the New Inn. In the distance behind the advertising hoardings can be seen Nazareth House.

Outing of the Kings Arms Saloon Bar Dart Club, 1955. Among the regulars pausing for refreshment *en route* to Brighton are, from left, standing: No. 5 Laurie Dargon, No. 15 Len Ralph. Kneeling: No. 3 Fred Archer, No. 4 Billy Hearn, No. 6 George Cox, No. 7 ? Hearn. The charabanc of earlier days has given way to a motor coach and the dress is less formal (no hats!) but the annual outing was still eagerly awaited in days when car ownership was far from universal.

Worple Road Supply Stores, early 1930s. No. 14 Worple Road, on the corner of Magdala Road (to the left of the picture) was for many years a grocer's shop. The site was badly damaged by bombing during the war and, along with the old terrace of Magdala Road and buildings between Magdala Road and South Street, it was redeveloped in the early 1960s. More modern housing also called Magdala Road together with the Shrewsbury Walk precinct of shops and flats were erected in their place.

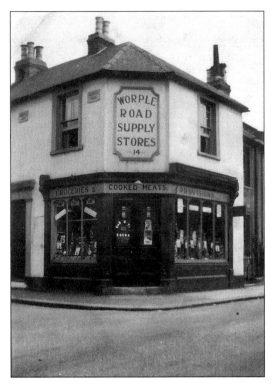

38 South Street c. 1930. F. Helsdon and Sons' tobacconist shop was founded by Frederick Helsdon in 1912. During the First World War Mrs Helsdon took over the shop while her husband served in the forces. Helsdon's is today one of the longest established businesses in South Street. Swann Court now occupies the site of No. 38 while the business has crossed the street to No. 35. Brands advertised include Wills Gold Flake, St Bruno Flake, Waverley Mixture, St. Julien and De Reszke cigarettes.

41

Interior of Helsdon's tobacconists, No. 35 South Street, *c*. 1960. They then advertised as 'Wholesale and Retail Cigar, Cigarette, and Snuff Merchants' and also sold all sorts of smoking accessories, even clay pipes. Left is Mr Chris Clayton and right Mr H.C. 'Joe' Helsdon.

William Winterborne (1836-1930) was born in Isleworth, and after serving an apprenticeship and gaining practical experience in various engineering companies he set up in business as engineer and iron founder at 79 South Street in 1866. A clever engineer, he designed and built a steam carriage in the 1860s which was later used to provide power in the foundry. He also invented a freewheel for the bicycle but sold the rights, to his later regret. To this day manhole covers and drain gratings marked 'Winterborne Isleworth' can be seen in many local streets. Married three times, he had fifteen children, some of whom helped in the business. He was a volunteer fireman, served on the Board of Guardians, the Burial Board, and as a governor for the Blue School where he had himself been a pupil. As a child he sang in All Saints' choir and throughout his life he observed the Sabbath, saying that he had 'very little confidence in any work done on a Sunday'. A teetotaller and non-smoker, he still worked, swinging sledgehammers, aged ninety.

South Street, c. 1907. Left is Francis Sadler's forge, next R. Watt's barber's – 'Stop here for an easy shave' – and, beyond, the canopy over Balch's butcher's. To the right advertising hoardings mark Mrs A. May's confectionery shop. The break in the pavement by the handcart marks the entrance to Wisdom's steam sawmill which lay behind the shops. In the distance can be seen the shops of 'The Pavement' and the turning into Algar Road.

Francis Sadler, blacksmith, wheelwright and farrier, ran the Forge at 80 South Street (see picture above); he is seen here in 1910. He was also a Freemason and Frontiersman. The business transferred to Kendall Road when the South Street site was purchased by the council for road widening. Sadler's shod the dray horses for Isleworth Brewery. Francis's grandson remembered as a child riding one shire horse from the forge to Isleworth Brewery whilst leading three others; for this he received 6d from his grandfather and ginger beer from the Brewery – this was in 1934. Children were also 'commandeered' into working the bellows for the forge.

The Clock Tower War Memorial, unveiled on 22 June 1922. The Memorial records the names of 386 Isleworth men killed in the First World War and also commemorates those killed in the Second World War. On the left is the edge of the old fire station, and on the right some of the shops in South Street. The sign on the end wall marks No. 82, 'W. Male & Son, Corn & Coal Merchants, established over 60 years'. Cereals – corn, maize, barley and bran, mainly for animal and poultry feed, were displayed in open sacks on the shop floor and samples of coal and coke were shown in the shop windows – 'Best Brights, 18/- a ton'. Deliveries were made by horse and cart, while sack trolleys could be borrowed by customers making smaller purchases. Next door to Male's the jutting sign marks F. Sadler's forge.

Flooding in South Street following a burst water main in the Twickenham Road, *c.* 1956. In the centre stands the Clock Tower War Memorial, unveiled in 1922, with Gumley House Convent behind; on the right is St Bridget's church. Wisdom Court has not yet been built, although the old shops it replaced have been demolished.

Two

Isleworth:
The Extended Village

*Gradually as Isleworth has changed from a village of Middlesex into a suburb of London so the
agricultural land surrounding the original village has been developed for the needs of the ever increasing
population – needs for housing, schooling, shopping and leisure facilities. At the same time the pace of
life has rapidly altered, the motor car replacing horse drawn vehicles, e-mail replacing the letter,
microwaves replacing the ovens, the weekly supermarket dash replacing daily visits to the corner shop.*

Gumley House, Twickenham Road, c. 1910. The central portion was built around 1700 for
John Gumley, a wealthy glass manufacturer, and two wings were added in the nineteenth
century. Since 1841 the house has been used as a convent with an attached school.

Art Room, Gumley House School, Twickenham Road, *c.* 1920. Originally a boarding school attached to Gumley House Convent and now a girls' comprehensive, the school is currently (1998) undergoing a £2.7 million expansion programme.

Twickenham Road from 'The Mount', *c.* 1915. On the right is the Catholic church of Our Lady of Sorrows and St Bridget. The tall building centre left is part of the Gumley House Convent and school. The low building at the extreme left housed the Isleworth fire engine between 1887 and 1937.

Isleworth fire brigade *c.* 1915. The fire station stood at the Mount by the junction of South Street and Twickenham Road. The station opened in 1887 and closed in 1937. Most of the brigade were volunteers who came running at the sound of the station bell. They had regular training sessions and took great pride in their positions. In the background can be seen the George Inn.

Butler's Almshouses, Byfield Road, 1960. They were built in 1885 to house two married couples and endowed by Miss Elizabeth Butler, whose father Charles was onetime landlord of the George Inn, South Street. A tablet in the porch records their erection as 'A thank-offering to God'. Elizabeth Butler died on 25 January 1904 aged eighty and further endowed the Almshouses under her will.

The Catholic church of Our Lady of Sorrows and St Bridget, Twickenham Road, *c.* 1915. Interior view showing the ornate marble Baldachino over the High Altar. The church was consecrated in October 1910.

Twickenham Road, 1914. On the left is the post office in Albion House, where the man is posting a letter in the wall box – a pillar box was later erected here. Next is the Duke of Cornwall public house on the corner of St John's Road and on the opposite corner is H. Martin's butcher's shop, where a hole in the floor gave access to the cellars, allowing meat to be thrown up to the shop!

Twickenham Road, *c.* 1925. Regulars from the Duke of Cornwall are ready for an outing in Daimler charabancs. Behind the awning is William Monks' sub-post office and tobacco pipe manufacturer (he invented a special pipe). Next comes the Duke of Cornwall on the corner of St John's Road. Today this busy junction is controlled by a mini-roundabout, but then there was time to pose for the camera in the middle of the road!

Twickenham Road, *c.* 1930. A delivery cart from Isleworth Dairy stands in the snow outside Sermons Almshouses, which were built and endowed by Sarah Sermon in 1843. Isleworth Dairy was run by Thomas and Alfred Bodger, cow keepers and dairymen, of 23 Lower Square, with 'Special Cows kept for the Nursery'. Their cows grazed on a field where the Blue School now stands.

Part of the Remembrance Day procession passing North Street on Twickenham Road in 1918. Behind the Crucifer are Girl Guides, pupils of Holme Court School, Scouts, clergy and choir, followed by parishioners carrying banners, then pupils of other Isleworth schools. In the background are Sermons Almshouses and the glasshouses of Silverhall Nursery.

Staff assemble at Isleworth Brewery before marching to the War Memorial for a Remembrance Day service in 1928. Those known are, from the left: 2nd F. Francis, 3rd S. Grey, 5th W. Irons, 16th W. Humphries, 17th E. Mitchell, 18th F. Humphries, 19th W. Butler, 20th E. Pocock, 21st A. Black, 22nd J. Butler, 23rd A. King, 24th A. Ford, 25th C. Smith, 26th T. Wright, 27th A. Lediot, 28th W. Heath, 29th F. Francis, 30th F. Thomas, 31st O. Phillips, 32nd J. Hibbert and 33rd W. Ross.

Entrance to the Isleworth Brewery, then run by Watneys, in St John's Road with the Brewery Manager's house in the background, *c.* 1960. Today this is the entrance to the Maltings estate, with a pillar box added on the bridge and a mini-roundabout to control the St John's Road junction. The street names in the Maltings provide a link to the past, recalling the Brewery dray horses – Shire Horse Way, Drayman's Way, Percheron Close and Clydesdale Close. If you follow the footpath beside the Duke of Northumberland's River through the Maltings you can still see, set into the banks, stone boundary markers of previous owners of the land: 'J. & C. Farnell 1842' for the Farnells, owners of the Brewery, and 'J. & C.H.S.: June 1855' for the Stanboroughs who once owned mills here. In addition to grinding corn the Stanboroughs made chocolate which was awarded prize medals at the 1851 Great Exhibition. The chocolate was sold for both drinking and eating: 'breakfast chocolate' (for drinking) at 6d per half-pound and 'chocolate bonbons' in fancy boxes at 1s, 1s 3d, 2s or 2s 6d each. They listed their address as 'Chocolate Mills, Isleworth'.

Isleworth Brewery, St. John's Road, c. 1960. Isleworth Brewery was formerly one of the principal employers in the area. A brewery existed in St John's Road from 1726 when John Atfield is recorded as owning a brew house. Various people owned the business, notably the Farnell family from 1800 onwards. In 1886 the business became 'Isleworth Brewery Company', which was sold to Watneys in 1924. Under Watney's brewing ceased on the site, which was developed as a bottling plant before closing altogether in 1992. The housing development called the Maltings and Atfield House nursing home now stand on the site, but the associated jobs – coopers and draymen, brewers, drivers and office workers – have all been lost.

Isleworth Brewery, St John's Road, c. 1960. This section of Isleworth Brewery stood opposite the Grainger Road turning, and housed brewery offices. Today the site is occupied by Atfield House nursing home, named after John Atfield, the first recorded Isleworth brewer in 1726.

Isleworth Brewery 'Fun Day', August 1935. Isleworth Brewery's Annual Fun Day of sports and competitions for the employees and their families was eagerly awaited and always featured a 'novelty'. Here we can see Beauty Queens Miss Heston, Miss Isleworth and Miss Hounslow – better known as Jack Saunders, Bill Cleveland and 'Snowy' Wells!

John Farnell (1778-1864) was a prominent member of the Farnell family who owned and ran the Isleworth Brewery in St John's Road. He was a notable local benefactor, contributing largely to the cost of erecting St John's church – the east and west windows are both his gift – and entirely funding the erection of St John's vicarage, Woodlands St John's School and Farnells Almshouses. He lived at Dairy Farm House in the Mill Plat.

St John the Baptist church, St John's Road, *c.* 1900. Sometimes referred to as Woodlands St John's. The church was consecrated in 1856, having been built on a site given by the Duke of Northumberland. The top-hatted, frock-coated figure is the Revd G.B. Stokes who seems to have liked having his picture taken – see below. The sender of this postcard has labelled it 'Church were [*sic*] Charlie sings'.

St John's vicarage, seen here around 1910, was built as the gift of John Farnell, owner of the Isleworth Brewery, in 1857. The building incorporates the Farnell coat of arms. Standing in the doorway is the Revd G.B. Stokes (vicar from 1890 to 1917) while his wife may be seen at the window. A smaller, modern vicarage has replaced the old building, which is now used as a boys' home, called St John's House. The creeper is gone and the drive tarmacked but the building remains largely unaltered.

Woodlands St John's Infants' School, 1902. Erected in 1859, the school closed in 1973 and is now a private residence. Log books record life at the school. There were pupil teachers and monitors to help the staff, the cane as punishment, absence through typhoid, diphtheria, ringworm and whooping cough. There was also disruption when snow covered the ground, when a circus visited the neighbourhood, when pupils were needed at home, when the schoolroom was needed for a bazaar or mothers' meeting tea and during celebrations for local and national events.

Farnells Almshouses, St John's Road, c. 1950. Built in 1857 by John Farnell, these provided accommodation for six men and six women, with a communal wash house and well to supply water. These have recently been modernized at a cost of £500,000, and re-opened on 28 April 1998. They are now leased to St Mungo Community Trust for people 'with mental health needs living in the community'.

A fancy-dress party at St John's parish hall in the late 1930s. Built on a site at the corner of Nottingham Road and St John's Road, the hall opened in 1925. It was used for parish functions, wedding receptions etc., and served as a polling station. The hall has now been demolished and the site is now part housing, part car park.

County High School, St John's Road, 1902. The St John's Road building opened in 1897, having developed out of the upper department of the Isleworth Blue School. In 1939 the school moved to Ridgeway Road, becoming Isleworth Grammar School. Note the four staff seated, wearing formal gowns and mortar boards; the third from left is the headmaster, Mr W.G. Lipscomb. The whole school appears in the photograph.

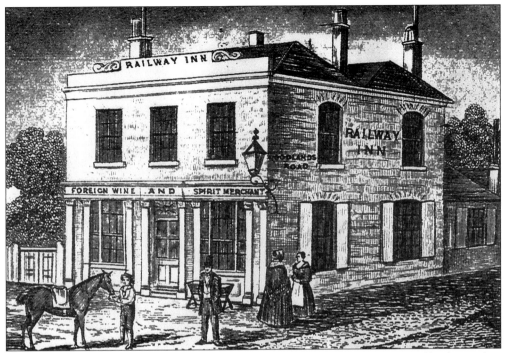

The Railway Inn, St John's Road, c. 1870. It was built on the corner of Woodlands Road in around 1850 for the Isleworth Brewery at a cost of £1,386 4s 3¾d including land, erection and licence. The inn has since been extended and the name changed to the Woodlands Tavern. In 1867 the landlord, W. Wickham, advertised that he 'respectfully informs his friends and the gentlemen of the neighbourhood that he has opened a quoit ground and bowling green for which he solicits their esteemed patronage'.

The garden of the Railway Inn, c. 1880. On the left is Mr John Chambers Jnr, who worked in a butcher's shop in South Street. In the centre is Mr William Wickham, landlord of the Railway Inn from 1867 to around 1885. On the right is Mr Nicholas Wotton, who worked for the Isleworth Brewery for some fifty-one years, eventually becoming collector to the company. At the time of this picture he lived in the Brewery House, St John's Road. He took a prominent part in local affairs, being a churchwarden at All Saints', a trustee of the Almshouses, a governor of the Blue School and member of the Philanthropic Society.

Woodlands Road, c. 1910. On the left is the footbridge crossing the Duke of Northumberland's River into fields where Octavia Road now stands. Through the gate lies the 28.4-acre field where Woodland Gardens was built, commencing in 1928. Woodlands Road goes round the corner on the right. Note the lamp post, also seen below.

Woodlands Road, looking towards Woodlands Grove, past St John's Lodge and Bedfont Lodge, c. 1910. Bedfont Lodge has now been replaced by flats of the same name. The road surface is still unmade but electric street lighting has just arrived.

58

Riverside Walk, c. 1900. At this time it was a footpath between fields and the Duke of Northumberland's River; the houses were not built until the 1930s. The Duke's River is a manmade waterway, cut in Tudor times to provide water power to the mills in the area. Wildlife still flourishes here; kingfishers, herons, dragonflies and butterflies can all be seen by those with time to walk. In the distance stand houses in Woodlands Road.

Octavia Road, 1953. Gathered outside Nos 17 and 19 are local residents who organized celebrations for the Coronation of Queen Elizabeth II. The second from left in the back row is Mrs Edith Woodland; three of her daughters also helped. In the middle row second from left is Mrs Alice Holt, and fourth is Mrs Palmer. Mrs Alice Mitchley is at the left in the front row.

Octavia Road, 1953. Children from the Worton Road estate enjoy a street party in honour of the Coronation. Following tea, local amateur entertainers provided amusements for the children. The Coronation gave people an excuse to forget, however briefly, the post-war austerity measures.

St John's Road, 1922. From the right the shops are: G. Hibbert's butchers, then W. Bowler's newsagents advertising Gold Flake cigarettes, St Julian tobacco and F. & J. Smith's Glasgow Mixture; next is R. Were's laundry and H. Hussey's grocers on the corner of Aylett Road. On the opposite corner is E. Parsons, another grocers, then A. Carter's greengrocers, Mrs E. Lisney's dining room and F. Penny's grocers on the corner of Woodlands Road. In the distance can be seen the Railway Inn and St John's church tower.

Mr and Mrs Alfred Carter in the doorway of their 'High Class Fruiterer and Florist' shop, c. 1910. Fresh fruit and vegetables, mostly local grown, were only available in season, though a few luxuries were imported – one bunch of bananas and five of grapes can be seen. Alfred Carter had several shops in the area, moving in around 1920 from 6 Linkfield Road to 23 St John's Road where the business continued under his daughter Lily until it closed in 1992.

Aylett Road, 1920s. Today, although the houses are largely unaltered, the road can scarcely be seen for parked cars. The Victorian builders could not anticipate the needs of the motor car and there is no provision for off-street parking – a prerequisite for any modern development. The pavement was not laid here until the 1920s – note the unmade road surface.

St John's Road railway bridge, *c*. 1960. Always a problem for high vehicles, this necessitated the routing of double decker No. 37 buses via Loring Road. Between 1990 and 1996 alone, eighteen vehicles hit the bridge, making it one of Railtrack's top thirty 'bashed bridges'. Today the bridge is painted in warning colours and the underside sheathed in steel sheets. Bricks in the bridge marked WFW 1849 and HF 1849 record the date of erection and former ownership of land.

The closing down sale of King's Hardware Stores at the corner of St John's Road and Loring Road, 1970s. This parade of shops, known as Cowan Terrace, was built by M. Cowan in 1931. Previously, part of the site had been used by Hibbert's the butchers of 13 St John's Road to keep chickens, selling their newly laid eggs in the shop.

Corner of St John's Road and Loring Road, 1962. Among advertising boards on Tolly's Stores one for premium bonds proclaimed 'Top Prizes £5,000' – somewhat different from today's multi-million pound lottery. In 1926 this shop was owned by Robert Salter who was also landlord of the Chequers inn. He had local orchards and sold apples at 1d a bag.

Loring Road, late 1950s. Double decker No. 37 buses en route from Hounslow to Peckham used this side road to avoid the low railway bridge in St John's Road, before the route was converted to single deckers. Increases in traffic and parked cars frequently delayed the buses here. Castle Road junction, in the centre, now has a road table to calm traffic.

First Isleworth Girl Guides, 1923. Beatrice Meacock and Ivy Hawkins, both of Castle Road, are in uniform as members of the company, which was attached to All Saints' church. Though more formal in dress and behaviour than today's Guides, they had no less fun then.

Visitors' Day at the company camp of the 1st Isleworth Girl Guides in Finchdean, Sussex, in the 1920s. A number of parents have travelled down to see their daughters. Note the delivery van from O.M. Lillyman, the butcher of 479 London Road, Isleworth, who was visiting the camp.

Numbers 14-38 Linkfield Road, *c.* 1960. Officially 'Bounty Cottages', but locally called 'Whitewash Alley', they stood at right angles to Linkfield Road, almost opposite Loring Road and were demolished soon after this photograph was taken, being replaced by modern houses and garages. Early this century No. 14 was a shop run by Mrs Coleman; here one could take a dish to purchase a pennyworth of jam. The tall building seen behind was part of the Pears soap factory.

Charles Arthur Figg's high class boot and shoe repairer at No. 4 Linkfield Road, *c.* 1935. The sign 'Best English bark used here' refers to the use of oak bark in the preparation of leather. An elderly resident recalls seeing 'Grandma Heinz', who was blind, sitting outside Figg's shop making pillow lace.

Mr. Reginald Corso in the doorway of his cycle shop at 6 Linkfield Road, c. 1925. Before car ownership became common, cycling was a popular pastime, as well as a convenient form of transport. Many cycling clubs were formed with both road races and time trials as common events. Shops like this sold both machines and spare parts and frequently hired out cycles as well. Today the shop has been converted into a house. In 1968 there were seventeen shops in Linkfield Road, including a butcher, tobacconist, two greengrocers, and four general grocers. By 1998 only four shops remained. There are, however, eight traffic humps!

Linkfield Road, 1953. Local residents in fancy dress costume process to the Town School where they were to enjoy a celebration tea in honour of the Queen's Coronation. Banners and bunting decorate the street and there is a holiday atmosphere – as one sign notes 'Reign stops Play'.

Children from Linkfield Road celebrate VE Day at a party held at Isleworth Town School, 1945. From left to right, back row: F. Tibble, P. Harvey, -?-, S. Johnston, B. Knowles, J. Tibble, J. Winch, P. Kemp, S. Battle, T. McDonald, A. Hearn, B. Hennesy, P. Fielder, N. Brown, W. Wilshin, R. Wilshin. Third row: R. Hance, I. Butfoy, J. McNeil, P. George, M. Cole, K. Young, B. Kingston, B. Lisney. Second row: -?-, V. Berryman, R. Spindler, S. Hammond, B. Flower, P. George, S. Winters, S. Johnston, D. Battle, C. Battle, T. Clutterbuck, R. Davis, F. Raffle, D. Battle, J. Waite, J. George. Front row: J. Fielder, D. Barfoot, -?-, -?-, -?-, R. Stanley, J. Brown, H. Haley, R. Barfoot, D. Lemon, -?-. The toddlers are unknown.

Isleworth Town School, Twickenham Road, 1957. Miss Tarrant's class of school leavers. Opened on 30 November 1910, the school briefly became a senior mixed school between 1928 and 1932, after which it reverted to being a junior school. In the early years boys and girls were taught separately and even had separate playgrounds, but by the time of this picture classes were mixed.

Worple Road School, 1912. No school uniform and only one girl wears glasses – an expensive luxury before the National Health Service. The school taught boys and girls, but boys had to sit separately from girls in class, a segregation which seems to extend to the school photos. The school closed in 1993 when the new Worple School opened in Queen's Terrace.

Worple Road School, 28 July 1927. Pupils stand together with Miss E.J. Chambers, who was retiring after thirty years' service as headmistress of the infants' school. Staff, parents and pupils gathered to witness the presentation of a set of hairbrushes and a gold watch, and to hear a number of appreciations and recitations by pupils.

Queen's Terrace, *c.* 1920. Among residents gathering for a charabanc outing are Albert and Sid Small, Mr Dancer and Emma Oliver. Advertising boards show the general shop run by Samuel Hosking at No. 15. A wayside war memorial was erected between Nos 11 and 12, but has long vanished.

Isleworth Town Football Club in 1930, following a successful season in which they won the South West Middlesex Victory Cup, and were runners-up in the Premier Division of the Hounslow and District League despite never losing a league match. Throughout the season they had played thirty-nine matches, won thirty-two, drawn five and lost two, with 135 goals for and only thirty-six against – no wonder they looked pleased.

Chequers Inn, Twickenham Road, 1933. First recorded as a licensed premises in 1731, the white fronted 'old' Chequers was demolished in 1933. The building behind is the 'new' Chequers erected to replace the old which was then demolished to provide car parking space. A sign on the wall informs that 'you may telephone from here' – a reminder of how few people had private phones at the time.

Twickenham Road, 1929. Floodwater has dislodged the tar-coated wood blocks forming the road surface, which has broken up under the weight of a heavily laden Foden steam wagon. Two trams travelling to Hampton Court have become stranded amid the resulting chaos. In the background can be seen the houses between Linkfield Road and the Chequers public house.

Percy House, Twickenham Road, 1916. It was built in 1883 as a residential school for workhouse children. In 1915 the building was converted for use as a military hospital, was subsequently used to house War Office records and then as an old people's home and was demolished in 1978. The site, along with the adjoining hospital sports field, has since been developed for housing – Ferneymeade Way, Town Field Way, Thackeray Close and Teck Close now stand here.

A patriotic tableau outside Percy House auxiliary military hospital, Twickenham Road, *c.* 1917. Britannia together with a tin-helmeted policeman, Scouts, a clergymen, Red Cross and St John Ambulance volunteers, a nurse and a 'wounded' patient pose for local photographer Stanley Nixon – himself a voluntary worker at the hospital. The nature of the occasion is unknown.

Thanet House, Twickenham Road, a late eighteenth-century building formerly known as Little Toolands or Keylands House and once home to John and Sarah Sermon (she founded Sermons Almshouses). The house was later owned by Henry Davis, a local farmer, and his family. The building is locally referred to as 'the Hen and Chickens'.

West Middlesex Hospital, 1920s. The children's ward prepares for Christmas with a Christmas tree, decorated trolley and covered lights (surely a fire risk!). Compared to today the walls are bare, with no murals, uniforms are formal, and the regime is far stricter with rigidly enforced visiting hours.

West Middlesex Hospital, 1943. Nursing staff and patients outside L1, one of the wooden huts used as a children's ward. The site is now occupied by the Marjory Warren Medical Centre. Much of the hospital is due for redevelopment in the next few years with older buildings to be replaced and facilities upgraded.

ARP ambulance, 1940. Attached to the first aid post at the Isleworth Health Centre in Park Road, the ARP ambulance was used to carry casualties to the first aid post which remained open throughout any air raids. The ambulance is seen here taking part in a procession raising funds for the war effort. Note the Borough of Heston and Isleworth's coat of arms on the door and the headlamps adapted to comply with the blackout.

Busch Corner, *c.* 1905. The London road faces Brentford with Twickenham Road turning off to the right between the hedge and the high wall. A large gas lamp marks the turning for late travellers. On the left the stall marked 'Spratt & Sons Isleworth' sold coffee and newspapers. The stall stood outside the field where the Green School was built. Compare with the picture below.

Busch Corner, *c.* 1934. The No. 67 tram ran from Hammersmith to Hampton Court between 1901 and 1935, when it was replaced by a trolleybus. Spur Road, to the left, was built to link Busch Corner and the Syon Lane junction on the Great West Road, coming into use in 1923. The parade of shops opened early in the 1930s. Busch Corner takes its name from John Busch (onetime gardener to Catherine the Great), who once lived nearby.

GREEN SCHOOLS.

Green School, Busch Corner, 1906. On 16 January 1906 the Duke of Northumberland opened these new school buildings, which consisted of an assembly hall with four classrooms, each accommodating thirty girls, set in two acres of playing fields. Today the school occupies the same site although it has been much expanded and altered over the years.

Green School pupils, 1905. The origins of the Green School can be traced to a Sunday school in 1796. In 1905 the school occupied premises built in 1859 in Park Road adjoining the churchyard. The building is now a private residence. Seated third from left is Sara Hayden.

Mr and Mrs Olwin stand outside Busch Corner Off Licence at No 146 London Road, *c.* 1935. There were no canned drinks then, only bottles, many with a returnable deposit to encourage recycling. There are no security grills either – only sun blinds.

Smallberry Green Secondary Modern School, London Road, 1947. It was built in 1939 as Smallberry Green Senior School. The school's original houses were named after local factories – Pears, Firestones, Gillette and Pyrene. In 1968 the school again changed name becoming Syon Upper School for Boys. Following the merger of Syon and Isleworth Grammar School, the London Road site was eventually developed to provide housing (Turnpike Way) and a new primary school.

Alton Close, 1945. Residents from Alton Close and surrounding streets gather to celebrate VE Day. Among the ninety-three people present are: Dawn McNeil, Joy McNeil, ? Hammond, Roy Hammond, David Booker, Mary Russell, Maureen Parker, Sylvia Knight, Valerie Cripps, Sylvia Baker, Jennifer Wincote, Gillian Hay, Eddie Baker, Peter Wincote, Bobby Cherry, Douglas Cherry, Marion Easton, Raymond Perkins, Pamela Lily, Jean Cheeseman, Mrs Howard, Paul Howard, Joan Hammond, Mrs Howe, Rita Fuller, Penelope Deighton, Alan Page, Mrs Edith Easton, John Walker, Joan Hey, Jimmy Wilkinson, Sheila Brooks, Dorothy Howe, Joyce Howard, Ann Page, Margaret Perkins, Jacqueline Prosser, Bob Hey, Mrs Hoare, Mrs Hammond, Mr Craig, Mr Tom Perkins, Mrs Parker, Mr H. Holland, Miss Floss Holland, Mrs Perkins, David Walker, Stuart Cherry, Mrs Cherry, Fred Prosser, Mr Stanley Hey, Mr Bill Hoare, Mrs Page, Mr Malcolm, Mrs McKie, Mr Cherry, Mrs Dorothy Prosser, Mrs Cripps, Mr Howe, Mrs Cheeseman, Ted Cheeseman, Gordon Malcolm, Mrs Morley, Margaret Malcolm, Mrs Wincote, Mr Brooks, Mrs Malcolm, Mrs Hey, Bill Cheeseman, Mr Wincote and Ronald Hyam (No. 12, seated) who became a Fellow of Magdalene College, Cambridge, and wrote *A History of Isleworth Grammar School*.

The Castle Inn, c. 1900. The Castle Inn stood on the north side of the London Road opposite Pears soap factory and was built in 1598. The inn closed in 1924, becoming a dry-cleaning shop before finally being demolished in 1961. The inn was very popular with travellers on this busy road and provided good stabling and coach houses.

Workers packing bacon at T. Wall and Sons (Meat and Handy Goods) Ltd, c. 1963. Wall's was one of a number of companies which occupied parts of the old Pears soap factory site on the London Road at various times. It was here that Wall's developed their pre-packed foods. Staff individually packed, sealed, weighed and priced packets of bacon by hand. Previously grocers would have had a side of bacon and cut it as required. Sixth from left is Kit Frost and seventh is Ena Field.

The laboratory at Pears soap factory, London Road, 1953. Among these white-coated workers is Mr S. Turner (extreme right). In 1789 Andrew Pears came to London to work as a hairdresser. He made and sold beauty products and eventually produced the transparent soap which made 'Pears' a household name. The business expanded and a site was purchased on the north side of the London Road at Isleworth where the 'Lanadron' works were built in 1862. Subsequently further factories were built between 1880 and 1884 on the south side of the London Road, known as Orchard and Primrose works. Pears continued to be run as a family firm under Francis, a grandson of the founder, and his son and son-in-law – Andrew Pears and Thomas Barrett – before becoming a limited company in 1892. In 1914 Pears became part of Lever Brothers, now Unilever. Production ceased at Isleworth in 1962 and Pears soap is no longer made in this country. It was Thomas Barrett who was responsible for much of the success of Pears and he has been described as the 'father of modern advertising'. He realized the impact of advertising posters and commissioned or adapted works by many famous artists; 'Bubbles' by Millais is still universally recognized. Barrett was an early proponent of adverts featuring endorsements of the famous, for example Lily Langtry. Barrett was also responsible for one of the earliest advertising gimmicks, circulating 250,000 French ten-centime pieces over-stamped Pears; these were then accepted as legal tender – and no law forbade defacing foreign coins. More recent 'advertisements' have included the 'Pears Cyclopaedia' and 'Miss Pears' competition. The most prominent member of the family locally was Andrew Pears, great grandson of the firm's founder. He lived at Spring Grove House, was involved in local politics, contributed generously to many local charities and organizations and had Pears Fountain built. He is buried in Park Road Cemetery.

Empire Day, *c.* 1905. Spectators watch races being held on Pears Field (now Sidmouth Avenue), although some seem more interested in the photographer. Held on 24 May to honour Queen Victoria's birthday, Empire Day was treated as a general holiday celebrated with great patriotism throughout the country. The crowds have turned out in their best clothes – and where did they get those hats?

Hounslow Model Laundry, 659 London Road, 1922. Despite the name this business stood on the London Road in Isleworth. Before the advent of washing machines and launderettes people relied on the services of laundries or hand-washed at home – Monday generally being wash day for housewives since cold meat left from the Sunday roast meant less cooking that day. A 1925 advert invites: 'Send us a few collars and compare the results with your present laundry'.

Three
Spring Grove, Osterley and Wyke

Sandwiched between the London Road and the Osterley House Estate, the areas of Spring Grove, Osterley and Wyke are largely residential in nature. Many of the roads were laid out in the 1850s when Henry Daniel Davies purchased the Spring Grove Estate and began to develop housing for the prosperous Victorian middle classes. Further development followed the opening of the Great West Road in 1925.

Spring Grove Secondary School, 1925. In 1922 the Middlesex County Council purchased Spring Grove House which opened as Spring Grove Secondary School in 1923. Generations of pupils passed through this hall before the school – by then Spring Grove Grammar – moved to Lampton in 1959.

Spring Grove Secondary School, 1925. Apart from academic subjects the school taught music, art, gardening, domestic science, PE and woodwork. Mr W. Cross, who was in charge of both PE and woodwork, retired in 1947 after twenty-four years' service. Note that short trousers were still being worn by secondary school pupils.

Spring Grove House, c. 1925. Once the home of Sir Joseph Banks, in 1850 the estate was sold to Henry Daniel Davies who developed much of the land for housing. The house itself later became the home of Andrew Pears, the soap manufacturer and, by the time of the picture, Spring Grove Secondary (later Grammar) School. Today the building is part of West Thames College.

Pears Fountain, *c.* 1900. Standing at the junction of Spring Grove Road and London Road, Pears Fountain was erected by Andrew Pears the soap manufacturer, who lived in nearby Spring Grove House. The opening ceremony on 19 June 1899 was performed by Lady Jersey who turned on the water and took the first drink. The inscription reads: 'This fountain was presented to the inhabitants of Heston and Isleworth for public use by Andrew Pears, JP, CA, AD 1899'. The fountain was removed in 1937 when it was found to cause traffic congestion. Behind is Charles Fenn's shop at 1 Clifton Road. His shop front advertises 'Cabinet maker and upholsterer; blinds of every description made to order; French polisher, carpenter and joiner; new and second-hand furniture bought and sold; furniture removed and warehoused.'

The junction at London Road and Spring Grove Road, 1938. Opened on 20 March 1937 by Alderman A. Bergin, the then central fire station of the borough of Heston and Isleworth cost £30,155 to build. It replaced the old fire station by the Mount in the Twickenham Road. The building was later extended up Spring Grove Road providing on-site accommodation for the station staff. Note that Pears Fountain has been removed from the junction.

London Road, 1910. Pears Fountain with the shops of Pembroke Place, erected in 1887, is seen behind. On the corner is Archie Peters' confectionery shop with S.N. Virgo's cycle works and garage next door – 'punctures repaired in 15 minutes'. Tin baths hang outside G. Osborne's ironmongery, while the awning and billboards mark William White's newsagent. To the left of the picture stands a cart piled high with baskets from the local market gardens.

London Road, May 1962. A No. 657 trolleybus is en route to Shepherds Bush. Behind the wall was the Kingsley Nurseries and Kingsley House where the music hall star Albert Chevalier wrote the song My Old Dutch while staying with his brother Charles Ingle. The building to the right is Derwent Lodge and the entrance gates to Galena House can be seen behind the trolleybus. All these buildings are now demolished, replaced by modern housing.

London Transport depot, London Road, 1962. Built in 1901 for the London United Tramway Company, and enlarged in the 1930s following the switch to trolleybuses, the depot finally closed in 1962 when the trolleybuses ceased to run. It has since been used as a Post Office transport depot and currently as a storage facility. Note the circular turntable.

London Road, 1908. The Milford Arms stands on the corner of Thornbury Road, centre left, with the shops of Pembroke Place beyond the turning. The pillar box stood outside No. 3 Pembroke Place, then a sub-post office run by William May. In 1914 postal collections here were at 5.25 and 9.15 a.m., 12.15, 2.25, 4.45, 6.30, 7.45, 9.15, and 10.40 p.m. – nine collections daily! The street still had gas lighting.

Spring Grove Central School, Thornbury Road, *c*. 1934. Pupils proudly pose with a selection of sports trophies. Competition, both academic and sporting, was encouraged between schools and within schools, which were divided into 'houses' – those at Spring Grove being Bulstrode, Gresham, Talbot and Waller. Extreme right on the back row is headmaster G.E. Bate, author of *And So Make a City Here*, a history of the local area. Also pictured are Miss Eva Shimming, Olave Dawson, Mazie Hughes and, holding the cup, Queenie Marsh.

Spring Grove Central School, Thornbury Road, 1925. Girls are performing the 'Jenny Pluck Pears' dance. Spring Grove Central opened in 1903 with separate departments for boys and girls. Classes of fifty or sixty were not uncommon then and even one of seventy caused only passing comment from a visiting inspector. The school closed in 1974. In 1998 the buildings have been demolished, and the site sold for housing.

Thornbury Road, c. 1935. The busy Spring Grove Road junction is now controlled by a mini-roundabout. The large house on the right-hand corner is Sherwood Lodge, with Stanley Lodge behind. Stanley Lodge is now demolished and the entrance of Stanleycroft Close in its place.

Milk cart outside 'Northway', No. 5 Witham Road, c. 1910. The buildings have fancy mouldings to set off the brickwork, and both railings and window bars are ornamental in nature. Each house was named rather than numbered – all factors designed to attract the newly prosperous middle classes when the houses were built. The milk cart delivered from Wyke Farm (see page 108), and proudly proclaims the patronage of the Earl of Jersey, owner of Osterley House.

Osterley Court, Spring Grove Road, 1909. Now demolished, Osterley Court stood on Spring Grove Road near the bottom of Gresham Road. It was built for the Taylor family, farmers of Scrattage, and was originally called Springfield Lodge, a name derived from the spring in the field where the house was built. The spring was said to have medicinal properties, its water being much used to bathe eyes.

Thornbury Road in 1923, facing south from outside the Osterley Park and Spring Grove railway station. On the right, the handcart stands outside No. 156, Bull Bros' fruiterers. Next door stands Sidney Abell's wine and spirit merchants on the corner of Osterley Avenue. Note the boy with his 'pram wheels' go-cart.

Campion House chapel, Thornbury Road, *c.* 1950. The house was built in 1856 for Henry D. Davies, who developed Spring Grove. Since 1919 the house has been used as a college to train men entering the Roman Catholic priesthood. The building was originally called Thornbury House, taking the name from the village in Gloucestershire where Davies's family originated; it was built as Davies's own home.

Garden view of St Tarcisius, Thornbury Road, *c.* 1920. Before becoming part of the Campion House complex, St Tarcisius was a private residence, having been built as part of H.D. Davies' development of Spring Grove. The building was a mirror image of Nantly House (see opposite).

Henry Daniel Davies (1819-1898). Born in Westminster, Henry Daniel Davies became a solicitor, but is locally remembered as the speculator who developed Spring Grove. In 1850 he purchased Spring Grove House and estate. Acquiring the Tryon Estate in 1853, he extended the property north to Jersey Road, west to Lampton and east to Wood Lane. Within this area he commenced work, laying out streets, planting trees and building large houses which attracted city gentlemen, those in the professions, and retired army and navy officers. Entrance to the private estate was by way of the Grove where a liveried servant manned imposing gates. New residents were encouraged by reduced rail tickets (Davies was a director of the railway!). As part of the development Davies personally paid for the building of St Mary's church. In the 1870s Davies lost much of his money through unwise speculation abroad and his planned development was never fully completed. Some of the original large houses survive, but many have been demolished. Davies was twice married and had eight children. He is buried in Heston churchyard.

Nantly House School, 1 Osterley Road (rear view), c. 1920. Built as a private house as part of the H.D. Davies development, Nantly House became a private school early this century. A 1919 advertisement promoted a 'High class school for girls, kindergarten and prep school for boys.' It offered 'sound, high class education on reasonable terms … gymnastics, fencing and tennis … healthy locality'. The composer Edmund Rubbra briefly taught here. Today the building has reverted to residential use, albeit with multiple occupation.

Cranmore, 8 Osterley Road, 1909. It is typical of the H.D. Davies houses built in Spring Grove and like several of the others this building has had different names over the years. In 1881, when it was known as Alfred House, the owner was George Holroyd, a colonel in the Bengal Staff Corps, who lived here together with his wife, daughter, six grandchildren and five live-in servants. The house was sold in 1893 for £1,150 to R.A. Harding – a window in St Mary's church commemorates a son, R.W.F. Harding, killed in the First World War. Later the site became St Christopher's Boys' Home. This 1909 postcard was posted at 9.30a.m. on 25 December for delivery the same day.

The Grove, *c.* 1935. The large houses on the outer curve of The Grove were part of the H.D. Davies development of Spring Grove in the 1850s. Those on the inner curve were added early this century. In the centre of the picture is Dudley House; Dudley House Nursing Home is now on this site.

Kenwyn, 40 The Grove, 1930. Built as a family residence, today Kenwyn survives, having been converted into flats known as Kenwyn Court. Naseby House, on the right, also survives with modern housing in Naseby Close now occupying the former extensive gardens. Other grand houses in the area have been demolished or adapted for different uses such as schools or nursing homes etc.

Wyndham Lodge, 24 The Grove, 1906. One of the houses built by Henry Daniel Davies, this was for many years the home of Miss Elizabeth Burton. Early this century the house became a school under the direction of Madam Beroud. Boys from the school would be sent to play on the 'Common' (rough ground between St Mary's church and St Mary's Crescent where the Great West Road now runs) under the supervision of an usher – 'a tall fellow who always wore a frock coat and striped trousers, with a bowler hat'. The house ceased to be a school in 1953.

Diabolo Drill, Spring Grove High School, 1908. From the earliest development of Spring Grove the area has been home to a number of private schools: Burlington Lodge Academy (a 'Gentlemen's Boarding School'), Nantly House School and Wyndham Lodge School for example. More obscure was Spring Grove High School which seems to have been a sister school to Wyndham Lodge, being run by the same principal, Madame Beroud. The school was possibly in Beverleys in Thornbury Road. Diabolos were a popular entertainment early this century, but are not normally associated with school games.

Porch House, 50 The Grove, 1908. This stood on the corner of Grove Road and is now demolished, being replaced by two modern houses. It was here in 1919 that Clive R. Fenn wrote *Middlesex to Wit*, an account of the Middlesex war hospitals. He had moved here with his mother from Syon Lodge following the death of his father, the novelist G.M. Fenn.

Odeon Parade, London Road, 1961. The Odeon cinema complex was designed by George Coles and opened on 20 March 1935 by the Mayor, Councillor C.L. Lewis. The cinema could seat 1,600 people, this being the heyday of cinema attendance. The first performance was *Crime without Passion* starring Claude Raines. By the late 1950s cinema audiences were shrinking as people had increasing access to television and the Odeon closed on 5 January 1957 with a final performance of Bob Hope's comedy *That Certain Feeling*. Roy Moore subsequently took over the Odeon for use as a store house, although the seven shops in Odeon Parade continued to trade. To the left of the picture is the junction of Harvard Road and further along, by the side of the trolleybus, can be seen the ornate gateposts which stood at the corner of The Grove. These gates formerly marked the entrance to the Spring Grove Estate and were erected when Henry Daniel Davies was developing houses on the estate in the 1850s. The posts were removed in 1965 to facilitate road widening, the gates having long previously been removed. To the right of the picture, next to the Shell garage, advertising hoardings stand in front of the copse where developers have recently built twelve four-bedroomed town houses called Fairfax Place.

Avenue Road in 1910, showing some of the turn-of-the-century housing erected between the older, larger houses of Spring Grove. At the end of the road is Avenue Lodge in Grove Road, formerly called Favilla Road. Avenue Lodge was described in 1897 as a 'bijou detached modern residence' it was then let at £60 per year.

London Road, c. 1965. Borough Road College students' Rag parade turns from College Road into the London Road. Students' Rag weeks, raising money for various charities, have been annual events for many years. The house on the left is Myfyrion, No. 454 London Road, and that on the right is Beechen Cliff, No. 452 London Road, both now demolished.

Numbers 456, Clydesdale House, and 454, Myfyrion (part demolished), on the corner of College Road and London Road, 1968. Both houses were demolished to make way for more modern flats called Thurza Court. Dr Bransby Yule practised for many years in Clydesdale House and William P. Williams lived at Myfyrion.

Numbers 1, 3 and 5 College Road, 1915. On the right is Henley House; Henley Close now occupies this site. In the centre is Bathurst Lodge, now demolished and replaced with more modern housing. On the left is Pelham Lodge, formerly Pelham House School for boys and at the time of this picture used as a Church Army Temperance Home for sixteen women 'suffering from inebriety'.

College Road seen from the Highfield Road junction looking towards Borough Road College. in 1905. The open fields either side of the road were developed for housing in the 1920s and 1930s and a war memorial to Borough Road College students and tutors was added at the Borough Road junction, but here the scene is still very rural.

Borough Road College from the sports field, 1906. The collage was built in 1867 as London International College, a boarding school for boys. In 1890 a teacher training college moved to the site from Borough Road, Southwark, and to avoid confusion the street was renamed Borough Road, Osterley, having previously been called Stanley Avenue. Today this is part of Brunel University College.

Borough Road College, 1912. Drawings of college life by a student were reproduced as a picture postcard. Sports have always played an important part in college life and football, rugby, rowing, billiards, hurdling and cross country racing – shown as a paper-chase – all feature on the card. Tennis, hockey, fencing and tug-of-war were also played. A pillow fight and toast in the dormitory suggest some enjoyable moments. But life was not all play as the pile of books and the student preparing for an examination show. 'George's Horse', the college celebrity, was the horse used to pull the mower on the college sports ground. The caption says it all: 'Pleasant memories of Borough Road'.

Borough Road College sports field, 1913. Many of the students from Borough Road College had teaching practice in local schools. Another link with local schools was the use of the college sports field for the school sports days. Here pupils from Spring Grove Primary School rest before a race. Seated fifth from left is Grace Russell.

Great West Road, 1929. Opened on 30 May 1925 by King George V, the Great West Road was originally constructed as a three lane highway becoming a dual carriageway around 1938. In the distance can be seen the Thornbury Road junction with the garage on the corner, and on the right the spire of St Mary's church.

St Mary's church, c. 1910. Consecrated in 1856, St Mary's church was built entirely at the expense of Henry Daniel Davies who developed Spring Grove. The east window, seen here, was added in 1864 by subscriptions from members of the congregation.

Osterley Court, Great West Road, c. 1935. This was a development of fifty flats erected in the 1930s, taking advantage of newly improved transport links in the area. Nearby Osterley station opened on 25 March 1934. In 1984 a plan to erect a further thirty-five flats on the communal gardens was rejected by Hounslow Council.

St Mary's Crescent, *c.* 1934. Development of St Mary's Crescent followed the opening in 1883 of Osterley Park and Spring Grove station in nearby Thornbury Road. The station closed in 1934 and is now a bookshop. On the right, light fencing marks where the bowling green was built, while the darker fencing marks the site of the present Osterley Library opened on 15 July 1966.

Osterley Bowling Green, *c.* 1937. Behind the Bowls Pavilion can be seen the louvred turret of the first Osterley Library, opened on 26 October 1935, with houses in St Mary's Crescent on the right. The present Osterley Library was erected in front of the original building which was then demolished.

Harewood Road, 1935. The opening of both the Great West Road in 1925 and Osterley Underground station in 1934 encouraged the development of new housing in the surrounding areas. Harewood Road was erected in 1929 by the builder H. Allen. The area was previously fields and orchards. The young girl on the left is thought to be Pauline Betts.

Marlborough Primary School, Quaker Lane, late 1930s. Pupils' games are supervised by Mrs D. Jackson, *née* Saunders, who was an international athlete and taught at the school for forty years. The original school opened in 1936 and cost £13,600 to build. In 1997 a replacement building opened on an adjoining site. This cost £4.6 million to build.

Marlborough Primary School, Quaker Lane, late 1930s. Mrs D. Jackson and pupils skipping. In the background is the footbridge carrying Quaker Lane over the railway lines; this was erected by the railway company in 1936 for the school's pupils and residents of the newly erected housing in the area. Previously pedestrians had to climb stiles before using a level crossing.

Wood Lane level crossing, c. 1920. Originally a manned level crossing, Southern Region of British Rail first proposed altering this to an automatic crossing in April 1967. Today the crossing is fully automated with closed-circuit cameras for added safety. Wood Lane can be seen on maps as early as 1635, although without any houses then.

SPRING DANCE FLOOR.

PHONE— HOUNSLOW, 2088.

"OSTERLEY" HOTEL,
RESIDENTIAL
FULLY LICENSED.

LUNCHEONS DINNE
TEAS.
FREE CAR PARK

Osterley Hotel, Great West Road, 1928. It was built soon after the opening of the Great West Road to cater for the needs of travellers. The hotel's ballroom with a sprung floor opened in November 1928, following a well attended supper and ball. Today this is the Osterley Four Pillars Hotel. On the left is the Wood Lane junction, with the walled gardens of Wyke House seen behind.

Wyke House, *c.* 1920. Standing isolated in large, walled grounds off Syon Lane, Wyke House was a fine building dating from 1778. Residents recall that it had a somewhat gloomy atmosphere, perhaps a reputation resulting from the building's use for many years as a private asylum. The building had previously been used as a boys' boarding school, but was originally a private residence and some of the interior decoration was by Robert Adam.

Indoor domestic staff of Wyke House, together with local policemen and a Chinese man (possibly a laundry man or cook), *c.* 1890. The house stood on Syon Lane, and at the time of this picture housed a private asylum. The house was demolished in 1977 and the site developed for housing – Braybourne Drive, Crowntree Close, Stags Way and Wyke Close now stand here.

Gillette's Corner, *c.* 1950. Designed by Sir Banister Fletcher and opened in 1936, Gillette's was one of the many factories to be built on the newly opened Great West Road bringing employment and prosperity to the area. In the late 1930s 900 people were employed by Gillette's alone. Previously the site had been farmland – Syon Hill Farm.

Wyke Farm House in around 1920, when the occupant was Mrs Elizabeth Ann Goddard. The floors were flagstoned, water was pumped from a well and there was no electricity until the 1970s. The farm was run by tenants of the Earl of Jersey, including in this century the Goddard and Goodenough families. Directories refer to the farm variously as Wyke Green Farm and Wyke Farm. Today the building survives as offices for Seccombes.

Wyke Farm, Syon Lane, *c.* 1925. This was one of many farms in the area providing both arable and dairy products for the ever-increasing population. Cattle and chickens are seen in the farmyard with the barn in the background. Horses were still the major source of transport and power, as shown by the various carts in the yard.

Wyke Farm, Syon Lane, *c*. 1970. In 1932 Wyke Farm was acquired by the Seccombe Bros' Motor Haulage Contractors who subsequently developed the site as a wholesale and retail builders' merchants. They still own the site today. Compare this with the picture opposite: cattle have been replaced with pipes and concrete and a lorry replaces the farm carts, but the 200-year-old barn still survives.

Osterley Park Lodge gates, 1915. Situated just north of Wyke Green, this was the principal entrance to Osterley Park and House from Windmill Lane until the building of Osterley Park and Spring Grove station in Thornbury Road in 1883 when the Jersey Road entrance was made. The lodges are said to have been designed by Robert Adam in 1775.

Osterley Park House, *c.* 1960. Built in Elizabethan times for Sir Thomas Gresham, Osterley Park House was much altered in the eighteenth century by the architects William Chambers and Robert Adam – some of his best work is at Osterley. Notable owners have included Sir William Waller, the Civil War general; Robert Child, the banker, and the Earls of Jersey. In 1949 the ninth Earl presented the house and grounds to the National Trust and today it is open to the public.

Osterley Park, *c.* 1915. During the First World War Osterley Park was used as a training camp by the Army Service Corps, where recruits were taught driving and vehicle maintenance. Similarly during the Second World War, part of the park was used as a privately run Home Guard training ground.

110

Four
Mogden and Worton

Small clusters of cottages with one or two large houses all set in acres of agricultural land characterized Mogden and Worton at the turn of the century. Today the picture is very different; the large houses have been demolished or converted from residential to commercial use. Much of the farmland has been developed for housing, while Mogden in mainly 'renowned' for the sewage treatment works which cover a large area.

Worton Hall, 1876. Built around 1873, Worton Hall had a succession of private owners until 1913 when the estate was acquired by London Film Productions Ltd and became Isleworth Studios. From 1952 to 1969 the site housed the National Coal Board's Mining Research Establishment. Today the hall remains largely unaltered but much of the estate has been developed.

Church of St Mary the Virgin, Worton Road, designed by H.S. Goodhart-Rendel and built between 1952 and 1954. The London Diocesan Home Mission first appointed a Priest-in-Charge in 1931, with services then being held in the adjoining building now used as a church hall. A notable feature of the church is the reredos of painted tiles depicting the Virgin and Child surrounded by biblical scenes.

The Royal Oak, Worton Road, c. 1900. This pub was first recorded as licensed premises in 1743. The house was popular with anglers fishing the Duke's River, with employees of the nearby calico mills and more recently by actors and staff working at the Worton Hall film studios. When this picture was taken the licensee was Robert Basson who was succeeded by his wife Catherine Basson. Contrary to popular belief it was not unusual to find women, especially widows, running businesses early this century – it was an economic necessity when there was no welfare state.

The Royal Oak, Worton Road, 1928. Compared to the previous picture, the building has been extended to the front and side and the upper windows have been altered; this work was done in 1921. The outline of the old building can nevertheless still be seen. 'Foreign wines and spirits' have been added to the ales and stout previously offered.

Oak Farm, Worton Road, c. 1900. Situated by the Royal Oak and for many years farmed by the Mann family. Note the wicker baskets in different sizes, and straw used to pack the fruit. The farmland has long since been developed for housing, and although the farm buildings survived until recently as a garage, they too have now been replaced by new housing called Christobel Close.

Congregational church in Twickenham Road, *c.* 1900. It was built as an independent church on the corner of Worton Road in 1848 and is now affiliated to the congregational federation. The interior of the church has been largely refitted, but the organ, seen left, survives. It was originally hand pumped, but was converted to electric bellows as the boys who worked the pumps occasionally fell asleep.

Isleworth Congregational church Boy Scout camp, 1922. Among those pictured camping at Cookham Woods, Buckinghamshire, are, from left to right standing: ? Salter, -?-, T. Chedgey; kneeling: -?-, E. Chedgey, -?-, ? Midgley, -?-, T. Fife. Note the bell tents, wooden staves and dixie over the fire pit.

Holme Court, Twickenham Road. Built in the early eighteenth century, Holme Court has had a variety of uses. It was initially a private residence, but by 1867 it housed an infants' school for pauper orphans from the parishes of St Giles and St George, Bloomsbury. In the 1870s and 1880s the building was a boys' boarding school under the Revd Thomas Slade Jones, who for a short period in 1876 employed the artist Vincent Van Gogh as a teacher. A blue plaque on the wall now records that Van Gogh stayed here. In 1891 the house became Holme Court Truant School run by the Chiswick and Heston school boards. This closed in 1920. Since 1926 Holme Court has been the headquarters offices of the L. Garvin group of companies.

Bear Honey, Twickenham Road, c. 1970. Mr E. Evans (right) is taking a sample of honey for Mr R.E. Morrison, director of the company and an authority on honey. Part of the Garvins group, the Bear Honey Co. Ltd was founded in 1923 and moved to Isleworth in 1926.

Christmas party at Redlees Retreat, Twickenham Road, c. 1930. Built in 1924 for Mr N. Greenham, the founder of the Greenham group of companies. In 1936 the house was purchased by the then Borough of Heston and Isleworth – including furniture and fittings, right down to pot plants. Some of the grounds were incorporated in the adjoining Redlees Park. The house is now used partly as an under-fives' play centre and partly for Hounslow's youth justice team.

Cleveland Road, c. 1935. The growth of Isleworth continued through the interwar years. Cleveland Road was developed on former market gardens in 1931-32 by Lonnon and Cragg the builders. Indications of increasing prosperity are the type of building – semi-detached – and the provision of driveways and garages for motor cars. Note the lowered kerbs for vehicle access and the telegraph pole indicating at least some telephone ownership.

Chestnut Cottage, Twickenham Road, c. 1890. This was one of several market gardens in Isleworth run by the Mann family. At the time of this picture the occupant of the house was Mr William Mann (see overleaf), together with his wife Annie and family. The names Mann's Close and Arnold Crescent – Arnold was the maiden name of Mrs Annie Mann – still record the family's link to the area, although housing now covers most of the former market garden land. Chestnut Cottage itself was demolished around 1930 and the land immediately around it was developed – Cleveland Road and Chestnut Grove now occupy part of the site. Pictured with Mrs Mann and five of her childrenis Miss Susan Button, who worked in the house and acted as nursemaid for the children. The photograph was taken by Mr Edward Hogg who was a professional photographer in Hounslow for a short period in the 1880s and 1890s.

Mr William Mann (wearing tie and fashionable bowler hat) supervising the unloading of produce at Brentford Market, c. 1890. Note the high-wheeled 'strawberry swing' cart, designed to be easy to manoeuvre on the farm land. Note also the initials W.M. plus the black dots on the baskets and boxes to distinguish them from those of other growers. The Mann family were prominent market gardeners in Isleworth from 1779 when three brothers arrived, having walked from Sutherland in Scotland. The family mainly cultivated land in the Twickenham Road, Worton Road and Mogden Lane areas. Principal crops included summer and winter vegetables, apples, pears, plums, gooseberries, red- and blackcurrants, rhubarb, pumpkins, peonies used to produce dyes, daffodils, gladioli, tulips, chrysanthemums and geraniums, the latter being grown in greenhouses. Produce from the Manns' market gardens were sent to both Covent Garden and Brentford markets, as well as being sold locally. In earlier days stacks of laden baskets were carried all the way by women, although by the time of this photograph this practice had died out. Like other members of the family, William Mann was prominent in local affairs; as well as being a major employer he was a member of the local council serving on the Education and Free Libraries Committees, he was overseer for the parish of Isleworth, trustee for the Isleworth charities and a governor of the Blue School. A pony trap used by members of the family can be seen in Gunnersbury Park Museum.

Ivy Bridge House, Twickenham Road, c. 1935. This eighteenth-century house was for many years the home of successive heads of the Mann family of market gardeners. The last occupant was Thomas Edward Mann who died in 1949 aged ninety. The building was demolished in the early 1960s.

W. & T. Mann's farm shop in Twickenham Road, c. 1935. Precursor of the modern garden centre, this sold produce from the firm's market gardens as well as pot plants and a few garden ornaments. Note the cold frames, greenhouses and sign 'Gladioli 2/- per 100'. The building stood near what later became the entrance to the Ivybridge Shopping Parade. This parade was demolished in 1997.

W. Mann's orchards off the Twickenham Road, c. 1900. The typical local practice was for the ground to be planted with fruit trees; apples, pears, plums, cherries, walnuts etc. were referred to as the 'upper crop' while underneath were planted raspberries, gooseberries, currants or, as here, bulbs These were refered to as the 'under' crop'. The sight of acre upon acre of fruit trees in blossom was unforgettable, but is now just a fading memory among older generations.

Heston and Isleworth sewage works, Oak Lane, c. 1920. In 1886 the Local Government Board approved the Heston and Isleworth sewage scheme at a cost of £77,000. By 1888 land had been bought at Mogden for a sewage farm and the first drains were laid. In the early 1930s operations at Mogden were greatly expanded as part of the overall West Middlesex drainage scheme. When this was completed in 1936 the Old Works at Mogden along with twenty-seven others in the country were demolished.

Five

St Margaret's

Situated between Isleworth and Twickenham, much of St Margaret's was in the ancient parish of Isleworth, and All Souls' was formed as a daughter church of All Saints'. Today, following changes to local government boundaries, St Margaret's forms part of the Borough of Richmond. Boundary House and Boundary Lodge on St Margaret's Road no longer mark the borough boundary – no doubt to the confusion of future local historians!

Maria Grey College, 1962. Built in the seventeenth century as a private residence, Gordon House has since had a number of uses: as a London County Council industrial school, as a girls' boarding school and from 1949 as a teacher training centre called Maria Grey College. Maria Grey College became part of the West London Institute of Higher Education, and later Brunel University College, and is still used for higher education.

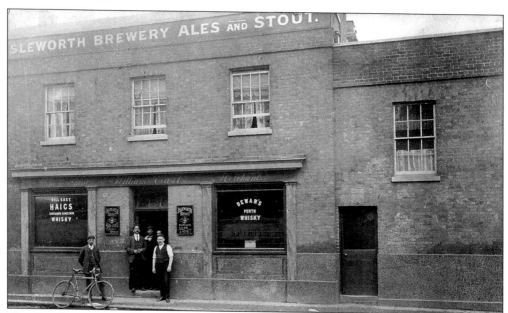

The Coach and Horses, Richmond Road, 1906. This public house stood between Railshead Bridge and Queen's Terrace. A picture painted directly on the chimney breast in the taproom depicted swans on Isleworth Ait. This was reputably painted by a customer who added to the work daily, receiving bread, cheese and a pint of ale in payment. William East, the landlord, stands in the doorway in shirt sleeves. Successive landlords were George Finn, Harvey Harris and L.A. Boyes.

The last horse-drawn delivery to the Coach and Horses from the brewery in St John's Road, c. 1955. Although altered in 1921 with a new frontage and bars, the building shows little change to the 1906 picture above. The building was demolished in the 1960s.

Kilmorey House, 1919. Built for but never occupied by the second Earl of Kilmorey, this house cost £16,920 in 1852. The Royal Naval Female School occupied the house from1856 to 1941 before moving to Haslemere. The house was demolished in 1945 following incendiary bomb damage and the site is now part of Brunel University College.

Kilmorey House, c. 1905. This was originally the assembly hall when the house was occupied by the Royal Naval Female School, a boarding school for the daughters of naval officers. Note the naval pictures on the wall.

Kilmorey Mausoleum. Built in 1854 for Francis Jack Needham, the eccentric Second Earl of Kilmorey who lived in Gordon House and had Kilmorey House built. The mausoleum was originally erected in Brompton Cemetery, but was moved to Woburn Park near Weybridge when the Earl moved house and finally was brought to St Margaret's when the Earl again moved. The building stands behind high walls facing the Richmond Road, and in it lie the Earl and his beloved mistress, Priscilla Hoste.

Ailsa Tavern, St Margaret's Road, c. 1900. It was built in the 1850s when the surrounding area was being developed. The name derives from the Marquis of Ailsa, onetime owner of nearby St Margaret's House. The cottage to the right of the picture was demolished around 1926, allowing a small single-storey extension to the tavern and the development of a beer garden. The road here has changed its name: early directories list the Ailsa Tavern in Richmond Road.

Northcote Road, September 1939. Members of All Souls' Church Lads' Brigade towing the bride and groom's car from the church after the wedding of the Brigade Major. Captain Ormiston and Lieutenant Reid walk by the car while among those in the traces are H. Mulready, G. Sadler and ? Randall. (sadly three of these lads did not survive the war).

Northcote Road, c. 1927. All Souls' church Mothers' Union members are ready for an outing. Designed by G. Monson and opened in 1898, All Souls' church replaced the temporary 'iron church' opened in 1886 and seen on the right, which was subsequently used as a church hall until demolished and replaced by a more permanent hall. Holding the banner is Mrs Emma Oliver.

Members of the clergy, church council, sidesmen, choir and servers from All Souls' church, Trinity Sunday, 1926. A large gathering at a time when church attendance was still general practice and social life revolved around church organizations and events. From left to right, back row: R. Brewer, S. Clark, R. Carnon, W. Clifford, W. Sharp, B. Inglis, R. Slatter, A. Pulsford, R. Moor, J, Sharp, H. Potter, W. Pearce, W. Madge, A. Mulley, A. Ormiston, H. Pellatt, A. Sharp, R. Sutton, A. Wilson. Second row: H. Hall, C. Brunt, F. Farrow, G. Bavey, C. Lambard, H. Lambard, L. Lambard, E. Lambard, S. Lewendon, F. Gasper, Major F. Murphy, G. Ormiston, O. Symonds, A. Webb, A. Tank, R. Turner, G. Meeks, T. Stoddart, C. Radforth, T. Robins, F. Radforth, W. Hughes, W. Pearce, T. Read, J. Stewart. Third row: Miss Hicks-Usher, Mrs Blewett, A. Hill, A. Lewendon, W. Evans, W. Marlow, G. Ross, J. Walsh, W. Lidbury, Revd L.St B. Milne , Revd E. Merritt, Revd L. Lewis-Low, A. Parker, S. Powell, C. Banse, J. Granger, W. Foster, Miss K. Keely, Miss E. King, Mrs Robinson. Front row: F. Rand, S. Blewett, E. Clarke, W. Curryer, L. Gould, J. Skinner, L. Widdrington, L. Perrett, E. Deckers, J. Pincham, H. Roberts, E. Moyns, H. Hill, E. Deckers, J. Hills, R. King, J. King, W. Gay, E. Stepney, A. Trollope and S. Osborne.

Numbers 30–34 Ailsa Road, *c.* 1915. Number 30, on the extreme right, was the vicarage for All Souls' church. The vicar at the time was Revd E.D. Merritt. Behind the wall on the left were the grounds of St Margaret's Lodge, now developed for housing. Note the horse-drawn delivery van.

The Lake Grounds, St Margaret's, 1908. Situated in communal gardens between St George's Road and Ailsa Road. The lake may be traced to one in the grounds of Francis Bacon's house at Twickenham Park in the seventeenth century, but it did not gain its ornamental shape until the nineteenth century. This idyllic scene could be miles out in the country.

St Margaret's Bridge, *c.* 1915. The bridge was opened in 1894 when a penny toll was charged to cross – hence the turnstile 'cages' at the bridge end. The toll ceased in 1938, and the turnstiles have since been removed. Providing you can negotiate the steps it is now possible to take a bicycle or pushchair across here.

St Margaret of Scotland Catholic church, St Margaret's Road, 1938. An offshoot of the Isleworth Catholic church, St Margaret's became a separate parish in 1930, with a new church (on the left) officially opened by Cardinal Hinsley in February 1938. Affectionately known as the 'Cardboard Cathedral', this remained in use until the present building opened in 1969, and has since been demolished.